Sadlier-Oxford

A STUDENT GUIDE TO

Writing a Research Paper

A STEP-BY-STEP APPROACH

PHYLLIS GOLDENBERG

TEACHER'S GUIDE
to
A Student Guide to Writing a Research Paper

Contents

Requests for permission to make copies of any part of this work should be mailed to :
Permissions Department
William H. Sadlier, Inc.
9 Pine Street
New York, NY 10005-1002

 is a registered trademark of William H. Sadlier, Inc.

Printed in the United States of America
ISBN: 0-8215-0770-2
23456789/03020100

Introduction

Managing the Research Paper Assignment

Like all English teachers, you are overburdened by too much content reading, literature, writing, speaking and listening, viewing, and language skills. There is never enough time in the classroom or in a semester to cover everything you need and want to teach. So how do you make room for the research paper assignment? Here are some strategies for handling the research paper assignment in your classroom.

Block Scheduling or Traditional Classrooms

Each year the nation's school systems are increasingly turning to block scheduling (90- or 100-minute periods with students concentrating on only three or four subjects a semester). In a typical classroom these extended periods are divided into three not necessarily equal segments of time during which students work at different activities. Block scheduling is perfectly suited to the research paper assignment. Once or twice a week, devote one segment of classroom time (perhaps the last period) to the research paper. Students can work individually, with partners, or in small groups. You might devote part of the research paper segment to text instruction, examples, and exercises; then turn students loose to work on their papers. If students work on their papers in class, they are far less likely to procrastinate, and you can keep an eye on their progress.

If your class is the traditional length—45 or 50 minutes—you have a number of options for managing the research paper assignment.

■ Students can use the book entirely or almost entirely on their own. It is easy enough for the average student to manage this outside of class.

■ Or you can work through most of the text in class, allowing time for partner and group work and keeping an eye on students' progress. Perhaps for the duration of the assignment, once a week you might focus all or part of a class period on the research paper.

■ Or you might use some combination of assigned homework and work in class. For example, students can be asked to read a chapter as homework and then do some of the exercises in class with a partner or a writing group.

Writing Groups and Peer Editing

Throughout the text, students are often directed to work with a partner or in small groups (three to five students) to discuss and compare their answers to exercises. Sometimes they are to complete an exercise together. Small group work is particularly useful in a long-term assignment such as the research paper because students advise and support each other through every stage. (Keep in mind that many students find the research paper assignment overwhelming and intimidating.) Group and partner work has the added benefit of developing students' speaking, listening, and social skills as they interact in an informal setting. Writing groups may remain intact throughout the time it takes to complete the paper, or you may form new groups every two or three weeks in order to give students a chance to know many classmates better.

Students are also encouraged to be peer editors, sharing and commenting on each other's work in progress. Although peer editing feedback is usually given orally and informally, you might occasionally use a written worksheet that asks students to focus on topics such as these:

- What I like best about this paper
- What I learned from this paper
- What might be done to improve this paper
- Questions I had after reading this paper
- Strengths of this paper
- Aspects of the paper that need work
- Tone of the paper

Individual Conferences

As students work through the steps of writing the research paper, keep tabs on their progress. Individual student-teacher conferences can be formal (3–5 minutes scheduled in advance at your desk) or informal (a stop at a student's desk), or both. Try to keep conferences uninterrupted, focused on the student's progress and on any problems or questions the student has. If you notice that many students are having similar problems and/or questions, you might spend some class time discussing the problems and possible solutions.

It is a good idea to spot-check each student's work at each of the following stages: choice of topic, list of sources, working outline, final outline, and first draft. These are the real trouble spots, when some students need both encouragement and prodding to move ahead. Be sure to tell the class when to expect your progress check so they have a chance to complete the work you will be checking.

Students of Varying Ability Levels

The text is geared for students of average and above-average ability in grades 9 and above. If you have students with limited English proficiency, modify the research assignment to a brief written

report of information or a brief oral report. Another option is to have students work cooperatively as a small group to produce a single paper on a topic they agree on. These students can go through most of the steps, perhaps skipping the niceties of documentation (Steps 2 and 7). You might ask a school or public librarian for help in assembling sources that students can use in class or in the school library.

Because students with limited English proficiency have difficulty writing and speaking standard English, consider teaching mini-lessons on some high-priority topics, such as sentence fragments, run-on sentences, subject-verb agreement, and irregular verb forms. Provide both oral and written practice for every grammar and usage mini-lesson.

Publishing the Paper

Students should proudly add their finished research papers to their portfolios. They might also include a brief reflection on their research paper experiences.

Encourage students to find other ways of publishing their papers. You might brainstorm some ideas in class: reading the paper to a school club or community club, creating an anthology of science papers for a science class, adapting their papers as speeches, etc. Ask each student for a photocopy of his or her final paper to use as a model student paper for future classes.

Before You Start

Before your students begin Step 1 (Choose a Topic), spend 15 or 20 minutes in class looking through and getting acquainted with the text.

Step by Step Through the Research Paper

Note with students that the text divides the research paper assignment into ten separate steps, or chapters. Take a minute to look at the table of contents to identify these steps. As they work through the text and its exercises, students are led through the various stages of planning, researching, and writing their papers. The end product (at the end of Step 10) is a completed research paper.

Each chapter is divided into "groups" of material arranged in the order in which students need to know the information. The teaching format is simple: instruction is followed by examples, which are followed by two kinds of exercises. First, students practice whatever skill or concept they have been learning on material the text provides. Then they apply the skill or concept to their own papers. Point out the post-it note symbol that precedes each highlighted rule (see, for example, page 7). Have students turn also to the end of chapter Checklist Review, which repeats each rule.

Using the Timetables

Have students turn to the timetables on page 137 and focus on the line that most closely corresponds to the number of weeks you have given them to complete their papers. Students should read across the columns, beginning with the first column at the left: 10 weeks, 8 weeks, 6 weeks, or 4 weeks. Reference to these timetables is occasionally made at the beginning of a chapter. Their purpose is to alleviate the two biggest pitfalls of the research paper assignment: (1) getting stuck at the beginning (choosing a topic or finding sources); and (2) procrastinating—not starting until the last minute.

Using the Appendices

If you do not point out the appendices at the back of the book, students may miss them entirely. Appendix A and Appendix C are useful from the outset.

Appendix A: What Every Research-Paper Writer Needs (page 138).   Go over the list of recommended "necessities": a college dictionary, a good thesaurus, a language handbook, and a book on style. Note that the text recommends specific titles but that other books are also available. Since students probably do not own a college dictionary, a

thesaurus, a language handbook, or a stylebook, try to make several copies of each available in the classroom. Show students where they are located and encourage them to use them.

Appendix B: APA Style; Footnotes and Endnotes (page 142).   Don't dwell on this appendix in your preview; there is time enough to deal with it when students reach Step 7. This appendix is included because some teachers (and some subjects) use a style of documentation other than the MLA parenthetical documentation style. Be very clear about which style of documentation you require students to use, and point students to the right pages in the text.

Appendix C: Writing Across the Curriculum (page 150).   This appendix is especially useful during Steps 1 and 2, when students are choosing and limiting topics and locating sources. Point out the lists of topic ideas and reference sources in each section: **Social Studies** (pages 152–154); **Science, Mathematics, Technology** (pages 154–156); and **Literature, Music, Art** (pages 156–157). This appendix contains other useful information about writing research papers for subjects other than English.

Using the Index

As students start writing their papers, they will want to refer to information they have come across earlier—but whose whereabouts they cannot recall. If you have time, have them turn to the index on pages 158–160 and make up a little practice drill.

Proofreading Symbols

Proofreading is covered in detail in Step 9. Proofreading symbols are displayed as well on the inside back cover of the text.

STEP 1

Choose a Topic

Choosing an appropriately limited topic is one of those trouble spots that can paralyze some students. A common problem is that students try to write about a topic too broad in scope. For that reason the exercises in this chapter give a great deal of practice in limiting broad topics. Students should feel free to change or modify their topics at any time during Step 1, but by the time they finish this chapter, you should have approved a final topic for each student. Occasionally, students are unable to find enough information when they start trying to locate sources (Step 2), so you might tell them that they will be allowed to adjust or change their topic if this happens.

You may want to pursue further the idea of inquiry-based research (see pages 150–51). Both teachers and librarians report that students work with more energy and produce better papers when they are re-searching questions to which they truly want to find the answers. Exercise 8 (page 16) asks students to phrase their limited topics as questions. You might brainstorm with the class as a whole some questions that really interest them. One student could record all of these questions (on the board or on a piece of paper to be posted somewhere in the classroom), which may lead others to topic ideas that really interest them.

Remind students to check the three lists of topic ideas in Appendix C: Writing Across the Curriculum. They may find a topic idea on one of the lists that leads them to a limited topic that they would really enjoy researching.

It would be useful to have one or both of these books in the classroom: *What Can I Write About? 7,000 Topics for High School Students* by David Powell (National Council of Teachers of English) and *10,000 Ideas for Term Papers, Projects, Reports and Speeches* by Kathryn Lamm (Arco).

Exercise 1

Brainstorm (page 9)

Lists of topic ideas will vary. Ask students to try for at least six topic ideas and to choose the three that interest them most. You might encourage students to share lists of topic ideas with the whole class.

Exercise 2

Making a Cluster Diagram (page 11)

The purpose of this exercise and the next is to give students practice in limiting a broad topic and then limiting it even further. To complete the empty diagram, students will need to use the critical-thinking skill of analysis (breaking down a subject into smaller parts). Their diagrams, of course, will vary. Before students start, make sure they understand that the diagram in the book may not "fit" their topic exactly; they should feel free to add or cross out circles as needed. You might ask students to exchange their finished diagrams with partners, who should be encouraged to ask questions about the diagrams and suggest additional limited topics.

Exercise 3

Limiting Your Topic (page 12)

The point of this exercise is to give students practice in limiting a general topic to one that is quite specific. Note that in the example on page 11 each level downward becomes increasingly more specific. Before students attempt Exercise 3, ask for a volunteer to do another example on the board. Suggest that students use the three broad topic ideas they selected in Exercise 1. Caution them that not every topic can be limited in three steps and that some may need only two. Ask partners to check to see that completed diagrams show movement from general to increasingly more specific. Have students share their final circles (most specific topic ideas) with the whole class.

Exercise 4

Identifying Appropriately Limited Topics (page 13)

1. **c.** Choices **a** and **b** are far too general for a research paper topic. Choice **d** is too specific—a single fact.

2. **a.** Choices **b** and **c** are too general for a research paper topic. Choice **d** is too specific.

3. **b.** Choices **a**, **c**, and **d** are all too general for a research paper topic.

4. **a.** Choices **b**, **c**, and **d** are too general.

Exercise 5

Limiting a Broad Subject (page 14)

Answers will vary. Here are some sample answers:

1. **Popular music:** pros and cons of censorship of song lyrics; how to write a rap; how Grammy awards are decided; how MTV began; how to copyright a song; origins of country music; how to succeed in hip-hop music

2. **Space travel:** American-Russian cooperation in manned space stations; NASA's shrinking budget; pros and cons of spending money on America's space program; cause of the 1986 *Challenger* disaster; what we learned about Jupiter from the Galileo space program; *Star Trek* warp speed—possibility or forever fiction?

3. **Cartoons:** a critical review of one episode of *The Simpsons;* a critical review of *Beauty and the Beast* (or any other full-length cartoon feature); women heroes in comic books today; how computer-generated animation works; the art of political cartoons; nominations for the Cartoon Hall of Fame (if one existed)

4. **World War II:** why America declared war against Germany (or Japan) when it did; Rosie the Riveter and other American women factory workers; eyewitnesses' views of life in Japanese-American relocation camps; the Munich Pact and its effects; what happened at Hiroshima

Exercise 6

Freewriting About a Limited Topic (page 15)

Answers will vary. Make sure that students start with a limited topic, not a general one, and emphasize that freewriting does not have to be in complete sentences.

Exercise 7

Revising Inappropriate Topics (page 15)

1. **My favorite Mexican foods**
   INAPPROPRIATE: subjective, not objective
   WORKABLE: Aztec influence on contemporary Mexican cooking; special foods for Mexican holidays; the history of chocolate; marketing Mexican foods north of the border (restaurant chains)

2. **Space exploration in the year 2050**
   INAPPROPRIATE: too speculative; probably won't be able to find enough material on the topic
   WORKABLE: Ray Bradbury's vision of life on Mars (science fiction); space scientists' predictions; the future of NASA and the American space program

3. **Airport security**
   INAPPROPRIATE: too general
   WORKABLE: pros and cons of two recent proposals to increase airport security in the United States;

the world's safest airports—and why they are;
matching passengers who actually board a plane
with their luggage—a complicated solution

4. **American Indian art**

INAPPROPRIATE: too general
WORKABLE: black-on-black style of modern
potter Maria Martinez of San Ildefonso; sand
paintings for Navaho chants or ceremonies

5. **Grammy awards**

INAPPROPRIATE: too general
WORKABLE: process for nominating and
deciding Grammy awards; detailed history of
a Grammy award-winning recording

6. **Hurricanes**

INAPPROPRIATE: too general
WORKABLE: who tracks hurricanes—and how;
what to do if a hurricane heads your way

7. **William Shakespeare's plays**

INAPPROPRIATE: too general
WORKABLE: two major themes in *Macbeth; West
Side Story,* an updated *Romeo and Juliet*

8. **Slang in my grandmother's day**

INAPPROPRIATE: hard-to-find material;
too specific
WORKABLE: African American origins of
slang words; the rise and fall of slang: three
case studies

9. **Chinese immigration to the United States**

INAPPROPRIATE: too general
WORKABLE: the Chinese experience at Angel
Island in San Francisco; Chinese immigration
and the Central Pacific Railroad; the Chinese
Exclusion Act of 1882

10. **Solar Energy**

INAPPROPRIATE: too general
WORKABLE: current developments in solar
energy; solar furnaces; solar energy and satellites

Exercise 8

Wording Your Research Questions
(page 16)

Questions will vary. Students might meet in small
groups to share their questions and suggest additional questions for one another's limited topics.

Exercise 9

Checking Your Progress (page 17)

At this point in the research process, students who
are having some difficulty settling on a topic might
profit from hearing how other students are faring.
You might have each student report briefly to the
class by reading or talking about his or her answers
to these questions.

STEP 2 Locate Sources

There are several ways of preventing students from turning in a "borrowed" research paper, one previously written by a friend or relative. (Unfortunately, research papers can be downloaded from the Internet and even bought in college and university communities.) One way to prevent students from turning in someone else's work is to spot-check work in progress at every stage. Another safeguard is to require students to use at least two recent sources in their papers. Ask students who cannot locate two recent sources, for whatever reason, to check with you for permission to continue with their topic.

Exercise 3 asks students to record and make notes of all the sources they explore. Encourage them to share discoveries of good sources with the class as a whole or with their writing group. You might have them turn to Appendix C, Writing Across the Curriculum, and see if they can locate some of the sources listed there. You might also remind students that they should not feel restricted to sources mentioned here. If appropriate to their topics, students might consider such sources as film, videos, scientific experiments, and other types of research.

Before students get started locating sources, ask your school's computer expert or librarian to talk to students about computer databases that they might use. If students do not have access in school or at home to computers and modems, try to give them specific information about where in the community (often the public library) they can go to use such databases.

When students do Exercises 5 and 7 on interviews and surveys, caution them about how to present their requests and how to avoid placing themselves in a possibly dangerous situation. As a general rule it is best that students interview or survey people they know. Make sure that parents/guardians know about and approve in advance any interviews that students schedule. Students should be required to submit to you index cards listing who is being interviewed, where and when (date and time) the interview is to take place, along with the questions they plan to ask. (Point out to students, however, that they should be flexible enough to follow an unanticipated "lead," should one arise.) Role-playing one or two interviews and then discussing them in class will help students improve their interview techniques.

To many students, bibliography source cards seem a waste of time, energy, and index cards. Demonstrate their usefulness by turning to the model Works Cited list (pages 135–136). Note that each entry on that list contains exactly the same information, written in the same style, as would appear on a corresponding bibliography source card. Once students have written the bibliography source cards, all they need to do is to alphabetize them to create their Works Cited list.

(Note that in this chapter and elsewhere in the text, underscoring rather than italics is used for titles in those contexts meant to illustrate or serve as a model for student work. It is assumed that most students will not have access to or be familiar with computer programs capable of italicizing. Those students who do not have such access and wish to use italics should be referred to a style manual for use of rules governing italics in general and in titles in particular. See also the Computer Connection on page 125.)

Exercise 1

Match That Source (page 23)

1. c	3. d	5. h	7. e	9. j
2. b	4. a	6. f	8. i	10. g

Exercise 2

Where Would You Look? (page 23)

Before students begin this exercise, remind them that they are asked to write at least one complete sentence. Answers will vary. Here are sample answers:

1. I would start by checking "dopamine" in recent issues of the *Readers' Guide to Periodical Literature*. I'd also look it up in an electronic database that has information that a non-scientist can understand. I'd ask the librarian for help in finding such a database.

2. I would check "hurricanes" and "weather forecasting" in encyclopedias, especially science encyclopedias. I'd also check a library card catalog to see if I can find a book on either of these topics, and if I did, I'd check their indexes.

3. I'd look in an encyclopedia under "Key West," "Florida," and "Florida Keys." I'd try the card catalog for the same three headings and look for "history of" as a subheading. If I don't find anything, I'd write or call the Key West Chamber of Commerce.

4. I'd check the past several years of the *Readers' Guide to Periodical Literature* under the headings "voting" and "voter registration." I might also call the local Board of Elections for information.

Exercise 3

Getting Started (page 24)

Lists will vary. If students are working on related topics, encourage them to meet in groups (a science group, an art group, a current events group, etc.) to share their experiences concerning sources. Those who are knowledgeable about computer resources might be able to suggest databases that will be useful to others in the group.

Exercise 4

Writing a Letter (page 25)

Before students write their letters, review the parts of a business letter: heading, date, inside address, salutation (followed by a colon), body, closing (followed by a comma), and signature. Refer to the letter on page 25 as a model. It is in the block style (each section starts at the left margin), which is the easiest style to type. You might ask students to draft their letters first on a piece of notebook paper so they can revise them easily. Finished letters should be neatly typed (or printed on a word processor) on plain white 8 1/2 x 11-inch paper.

Encourage students to use the telephone (and directory) to locate names, titles, and addresses for local experts and elected officials. They can find addresses for many famous people in *Who's Who in America*, published each year. Librarians may be able to suggest other sources for locating experts' names and addresses.

Exercise 5

Preparing for an Interview (page 26)

Questions will vary, and some students will have trouble drafting five questions. Ask them to try for at least four. Here are some sample answers:

1. **Name of Person:** (a professional tennis player)

   - How did you get started playing tennis?

   - What kind of training or instruction did you have?

   - What do you think is the ideal training or instruction for a young tennis player? At what age should training begin?

   - What do you think are the biggest mistakes that young people make when they start playing in tournaments?

   - What advice would you give to a young person who is seriously interested in tennis as a career?

   - If you were running a tennis school or tennis camp, what would it be like?

2. **Name of person:** (a local judge)

   - In the last five years or so, what types of juvenile crime are on the increase in this community? on the decrease?

   - Can you describe some programs that have been tried around the country to prevent juvenile crime? Which of these programs do you think have been most successful?

   - What specific recommendations would you make for preventing juvenile crime in this community?

   - What advice would you give to a parent whose son or daughter has been arrested for the first time?

   - What would you say to a young person who has been arrested for the third time?

3. **Name of person:** (a board-of-education member)

   - What are the board's short-range and long-range plans to relieve overcrowding in the schools?

   - What is being done to lower the dropout rate?

   - What are the schools doing to prepare students for the workplace? What specific skills programs and job-training programs exist now?

   - What can we students do to improve our schools?

   - Please describe what the schools are currently doing about drug education (from elementary school through high school).

   - If you could have all the money you needed, what specific programs would you like to see the schools adopt? Which of these programs do you consider most important?

Exercise 6

Focusing on Your Community (page 27)

Answers will vary. Sample answers are given, but names and addresses will vary. You might use this activity as the springboard for having students compile a directory of local sources of information. Keep the directory as a classroom resource for future classes but be sure to have a committee verify information and update it each year.

1. I'd look in the telephone book and call the city's and/or county's Board of Education and the Parks Department.

2. I'd look in the telephone book and call the city's and/or county's Sanitation Department or Waste Disposal Department or Recycling Department.

3. I'd talk to someone at City Hall and ask about the senior services division. I might also talk to someone involved in a senior citizens organization, such as the Gray Panthers or the local AARP. Another source of information would be a social worker at a senior citizens home or day-care center.

4. I'd call City Hall and ask to talk to someone about where I could see a copy of the budget and about who decides how local taxes are

spent. I could ask a city council representative or someone in the mayor's office.

5. I'd ask the librarian for information, and I'd also try the local newspaper's arts editor. If I didn't find out what I wanted to know, I'd call City Hall and ask to speak to someone in charge of the arts program.

Exercise 7

Conducting a Survey (page 28)

Students' surveys will vary. Here are six sample survey questions:

1. How often do you spend two hours or more watching television?
   □ every day   □ only on weekends
   □ never   □ three or four times a week

2. Which of the following types of programs do you prefer? (Check as many as you like.)
   □ news   □ sports events   □ movies   □ music
   □ talk show   □ game show   □ educational
   □ situation comedy   □ drama   □ soap opera

3. What time of day can you usually be found watching television?
   □ morning   □ afternoon   □ from 5–7 P.M.
   □ between 7 P.M. and midnight

4. Who is usually watching TV with you?
   □ I watch alone   □ one or more friends
   □ one or more family members

5. Do you watch TV advertisements?
   □ yes   □ yes, but with the sound muted   □ no

6. How do you decide what to watch?
   □ I watch the same programs every week and know the schedule by heart.   □ I channel-surf.
   □ I check the listings in a newspaper.
   □ I use a TV guide.

Exercise 8

Go to It (page 29)

Answers will vary. Suggest that they share their responses in small groups. Those who are planning an interview might form a group; those who are planning a survey; etc. Students might work in pairs to complete a survey and report their findings to the class. Make sure that you OK their plans for interviews and surveys before they do them. Students may need permission from the administration before they can conduct a survey in school.

Exercise 9

Preparing Bibliography Source Card Entries (page 34)

Students should do Exercises 9 and 10 before they write their bibliography cards to familiarize themselves with the MLA style. Remind them that if they do their bibliography cards correctly, they will use the exact same entries on their Works Cited list.

1. Paul, Ellen. *Adoption Choices*. Detroit: Gale Research, 1991.

2. Bunch, Bryan, and Alexander Hellemans. *The Timetables of Technology*. New York: Simon & Schuster, 1993.

3. Pinna, Giovanni. *The Illustrated Encyclopedia of Fossils*. Trans. Jay Hyams. New York: Facts on File, 1990.

4. Hamblin, Dora Jane. "Neil Armstrong: He Could Fly Before He Could Drive." *Life*. 1969.

Exercise 10

What's Wrong with These Bibliography Source Card Entries? (page 35)

1. Hickok, Ralph. *A Who's Who of Sports Champions*. New York: Houghton Mifflin, 1995.

2. Tenenbaum, Francine, Rita Buchanan, and Roger Holmes, eds. *Taylor's Master Guide to Gardening*. Boston: Houghton Mifflin, 1994.

3. Allende, Isabel. *Paula*. Trans. Margaret Sayers Peden. New York: HarperCollins, 1994.

4. Hahn, Harley. *The Internet Yellow Pages*. 3rd ed. Berkeley, CA: McGraw Hill, 1996.

5. French, Howard W. "For Ivory Coast Women, New Battle for Equality." *New York Times* 6 Apr. 1996:4, southern ed.

6. Jerome, Marty. "Printers Get Personal." *PC Computing*. Feb. 1996: 140+.

Exercise 11

Exploring Sources (page 36)

Lists and bibliography cards will vary. It is a good idea to have individual conferences with students as they are doing this exercise. Students who—for whatever reason—get "stuck" at this point will need some advice about sources to keep their research going.

STEP 3 — Take Notes

If you save some student model papers from previous years, try to get student writers to donate their note cards, too. Ask writers to staple each note card to the back of the page on which the quote or paraphrase appears. The rather strange-looking result (a paper with many note cards stapled to each sheet) demonstrates how notes get turned into papers. As always, peer models are much more meaningful than abstract teaching. Have students break into small groups to examine and talk about these model papers and note cards.

You can create additional note-taking practice exercises either by duplicating passages from books or by using an overhead to project such passages. Give students a limited time (3–5 minutes) to take notes on the passage and then have them compare their notes with a partner or group.

Also, you can easily create note-taking exercises that will improve students' listening skills. Have them take notes while you read aloud a newspaper or magazine article or a page or two from a biography at the appropriate reading level. After you finish reading, talk about the notes they have taken. This kind of listening practice helps prepare students for taking notes in college lectures.

Exercise 1

Making a Working Outline for Your Paper (page 38)

Before students begin their outlines, spend some time in class discussing the outline form in the example on page 38. (They will study the outline form further in Step 5.) Note that the example on page 38 is a topic outline (no complete sentences) and that the paper's topic has been divided into three large subdivisions (marked by roman numerals I, II, and III). Have students note the further subdivisions: first capital letters, then arabic numerals, and, if there were an even smaller subdivision, lowercase letters. Note that a subdivision must have no fewer than two entries; a topic or subtopic can never be divided only once. Students' outlines will vary. You will want to look at them briefly (walking around the classroom will suffice) to make sure students' plans seem workable.

Exercise 2

Practice Skimming to Locate Information (page 39)

Answers will vary. You can give additional practice in skimming by asking students questions about information in textbooks they all have. For example, on what page (using the index) will you find information about the life of Langston Hughes? When was he born? Who was Simple? etc.

Exercise 3

Skimming One of Your Sources (page 40)

Answers will vary. Before students do this exercise, discuss with them the concept of "useful information." An encyclopedia—or any other source—is filled with facts. Make sure students understand that facts are "useful" only if they pertain directly to their limited topic.

Exercise 4

Taking Notes for a Direct Quotation (page 42)

Students' notes will vary. Look for the large quotation marks surrounding the quoted material, the heading in the upper left corner, the source card

number in the upper right corner, and the page number in the lower right corner. Students may want to add some explanatory notes of their own. Here is a sample note card:

C.S. Sulzberger on blockade   7

Sulzburger was the NY Times foreign correspondent during Cuban missile crisis.

"We have opted to force the issue ourselves without prior approval of our allies and there are going to be uneasy diplomatic moments."

sec 1:38

Exercise 5

Paraphrasing (page 44)

Answers will vary. You might have the students work in pairs to make sure they have not copied the wording of the original paragraph. If students seem uneasy with paraphrasing, give them additional in-class practice with a chance to compare and discuss their paraphrases.

Exercise 6

Summarizing Important Information from a Source (page 45)

For additional practice before students do this exercise, you might hand out to the class a page of factual text and have them all write a summary on a piece of notebook paper the size of a note card. Students can then work in small groups or in pairs to compare their summaries, or you might have a few read aloud and discuss what makes a good summary.

Note cards will vary. Caution the students to focus on main ideas and to be sure to include heading, source number, and page number.

Here is a sample note card from Edward O. Wilson's *The Diversity of Life*.

Destruction of species—caused by humans   3

Humans cut down primeval forests and rain
forests both for timber and for land development.
When forest ecosystems are destroyed, tens of
thousands of species die with their habitat. Wilson
identifies 18 "hot spots," forest areas in danger
of extinction from human activity. These hot spots
contain species of plants and animals found
nowhere else in the world.

pp. 259–269

Exercise 7

Practice Taking Notes (page 45)

Remind students that note cards contain both a
source number (at upper right) and page numbers
(at lower right), but in this exercise they will not
have either. Students' notes will vary. Students will
benefit from meeting with partners or in small
groups to compare and talk about their notes—
what they have included and what they have left
out. Here are sample notes:

Jackie Robinson's start in major leagues

Branch Rickey, Bklyn. Dodgers pres., decides to
hire 1 African American & chooses Robinson for
Montreal Royals.

1946 — Led league in batting & runs scored
4/10/47—1st African Amer. in major leagues: 1st
base with Dodgers; Rookie of the Year
MVP in 1949; 1962— inducted Baseball Hall of
Fame. 1st baseball player on U.S. stamp.

Exercise 8

Practice Taking Notes During an Interview (page 46)

Answers will vary. If time permits, give each student
a chance to introduce the classmate interviewed.
You might limit introductions to one or two minutes. This activity not only gives students practice
in interviewing and taking notes but also in speaking
and listening skills. Students—especially those who
are shy or new to the school—benefit from learning
about one another's interests and backgrounds.

Exercise 9

Taking Notes for Your Research Paper (page 47)

Note cards will vary. To make sure that note taking
goes smoothly, you might want to spot-check each
student's cards or have pairs of students exchange
and check each other's cards.

Write a Thesis Statement and a Title

Spend some time discussing pages 48–51 with the whole class. The concepts of unity and coherence are introduced here as tools to help students decide what information to keep and what to discard, but unity and coherence are all-important concepts in the writing process. Both should be reemphasized when students write their final outline (Step 5), when they sit down to write their first draft (Step 6), and when they revise that draft (Step 8). This chapter's rules on unity and coherence apply at every step.

Drafting a thesis statement and writing a title are the two easiest tasks in the research paper assignment. If you want to give students additional practice in revising faulty thesis statements and titles, assign small groups to make them up and write their best three or four on the board for class-mates to revise. Since the thesis statement, in a real sense, "controls" the content of the paper, you might want to spot-check students' final versions (Exercise 6).

Exercise 1

What Fits and What Doesn't? (page 50)

1. a. ✓ b. ✓ c. ✓ d. ✓ e. ✗ f. ✓ g. ✗

Exercise 2

Evaluating Your Notes (page 50)

Progress reports will vary.

Exercise 3

Ensuring Coherence (page 51)

Progress reports will vary. Assure students that it is perfectly normal to revise their plans for the paper in the light of the actual information they have collected. Encourage students to revise their working outlines at this point, if necessary. Working with a revised outline that accurately reflects their research will make the final outline (Step 5) much easier.

Exercise 4

Identifying Your Audience and Purpose (page 52)

Answers will vary. You might have students share their answers to these questions with the class as a whole. Stress that defining audience and purpose are an essential prewriting step for persuasive writing as well as expository writing (writing to explain).

Exercise 5

Revising Thesis Statements (page 53)

Answers will vary. When students have finished writing revised thesis statements, have them meet in small groups to compare and discuss what they have written. Sample answers are given.

1. Strikes by professional players have not only changed the character of sports in America but have also alienated once-loyal fans.

2. In the last part of the twentieth century, electronic mail—E-mail—changed business and personal communications as profoundly as the telephone changed communication in the early part of the century.

3. A recent study of 250 teenagers in MacArthur High School yielded several conclusions on the relationship between TV-viewing habits and school achievement.

4. If no counselor is available, a troubled teenager may find comfort and advice in an unlikely place: a young adult novel.

Exercise 6

Drafting a Thesis Statement for Your Paper (page 55)

You will find that having students draft alternative versions and evaluate them individually and in a small group of peers is an effective approach to many writing tasks. Students will use this same approach for writing titles (see Exercise 8), introductions, and conclusions.

Exercise 7

Revising Titles (page 56)

Answers will vary. Sample answers are given.

1. The United Nations and Its Mission to the World's Children

2. Encouraging Creativity: A Way to Grow

3. Last Season's TV's Sit-com Hits: Writing to a Formula

4. The Role of Special-effect Artists in Movies About Extraterrestrial Life

5. The Mysterious Last Days of Edgar Allan Poe

6. Eat Well and Live a Longer, Healthier Life

7. Teenagers and Their Cars: Statistics vs. Stereotypes

8. How to Write a Rap: Advice from Experts

Exercise 8

Drafting a Title for Your Research Paper (page 57)

You might note that the colon is a handy device but that not every title needs one. Ask each student to write his or her working title on a slip of paper, and display these on a bulletin board titled "Work in Progress." Or have students read aloud their working titles.

STEP 5 — Write a Final Outline

If students have done a working outline, this step will be easy. Everyone will benefit from working through all of the exercises, however. Exercises 1, 3, and 4 provide students with material; Exercises 2, 5, and 6 focus on their own outlines.

Before students turn to their own outlines, you might spend some time in class talking about types of research papers and the three patterns of organization (pages 151–52 in Appendix C). Discussing these methods of organization may give some students ideas about better ways to organize their papers. Confer briefly with students who want to change their working outlines drastically.

Exercise 1

Analyzing a Topic to Formulate Main Headings (page 63)

Answers will vary considerably. You might compare and discuss answers with the class as a whole. Students will benefit from hearing different approaches to breaking the topic into smaller headings. Sample answers are given.

1. **I.** New techniques for increasing registration
   II. Educating and empowering nonvoters
   III. Using the media
   IV. Proposals to penalize nonvoters

2. **I.** A brief history of electric automobiles
   II. Advantages of electric automobiles
   III. Disadvantages of electric automobiles
   IV. Predicting the future for electric automobiles

3. **I.** Live and continuing coverage of major news events and disasters
   II. Viewing sports events from the comfort of home
   III. Caring about the characters: a common interest
   IV. Watching old movies

4. **I.** What the ads promise
   II. Images that persuade
   III. Advertisements that tell stories
   IV. Words and music

Exercise 2

Identifying the Main Headings in Your Research Paper (page 63)

Although space has been left for five main headings, make sure students understand they only need to provide three. Answers will vary.

Exercise 3

Parallel Structure (page 65)

Answers will vary. Students might meet with partners or in small groups to revise these two outlines. Sample answers are given.

1. **Topic:** Jane Addams and her work
   I. Her life
   II. Her work at Hull House
   III. Her other work
      A. Women's rights
      B. Nobel Peace Prize

2. Topic: Animated cartoons: the technology

I. Hand-drawn cartoons

    A. Process of animation

    B. Earliest short cartoons

    C. Full-length animated movies

        1. Created at Walt Disney studios

        2. Created by "Nine Old Men"

II. Computer-generated animation

    A. Process of animation

    B. *Tron* (1984), first computer-animated film

III. Future of animation

Exercise 4

What Might the Headings Be? (page 66)

This exercise prepares students for the actual problems they will face when they try to create a working outline based on their notes. They will probably have many more notes than they can use. Be sure to explain that they need not include everything that is in their notes when they draft a working outline. Students will benefit from working either with partners or in a small group to develop an outline based on these notes. Answers will vary. A sample outline is given. If you decide to share this outline with your class, have them notice that the material on the origin of the word *skyscraper* has been completely omitted and that two headings have been added (Jenney's later work, Work of other early architects) that will require further research. Such additions and deletions are typical in the process of turning notes into a final paper.

Skyscrapers: Two Inventions That Made Them Possible

Thesis statement: Two American inventions— steel-frame construction and a safety device for elevators—led to the skyscraper, which altered earth's human landscape.

I. History of skyscraper

    A. Masonry construction method before skyscrapers

    B. Chicago fire (October 1871)

        1. Destruction of central city

        2. Building boom

II. Steel-frame construction

    A. Advantages over masonry

        1. More windows

        2. More room at base

        3. Greater number of stories

    B. History

        1. Chicago's nine-story Home Insurance Company Building (1884–1885)

        2. Architect Major William LeBaron Jenney

            a. Anecdote about Jenney's wife putting book on birdcage

            b. Jenney's later work

        3. Work of other early architects

III. Safety device for elevators

    A. History

        1. Invented by Elisha Graves Otis (1811–1861) in New York City

        2. Stopped elevator from falling if chain broke

        3. Patented in 1861

    B. Passenger elevators (1857)

        1. Used in hotels

        2. First powered by steam

        3. Later powered by electric motors

IV. Importance of skyscrapers

    A. Growth of cities

        1. Centers of commerce

        2. Urban density

    B. Positive effects

    C. Negative effects (Mumford quotes)

Exercise 5

Revising Your Working Outline (page 68)

Answers will vary. Have students discuss their answers with partners or in a small group.

Exercise 6

Writing Your Final Outline (page 69)

Outlines will vary. You will want to check the final outlines to make sure students are on a viable course. This can be done informally, stopping at students' desks for brief conferences. You might also have students share their final outlines with peers —either in a small group or by exchanging outlines with partners. Ask them to check each other's outlines for logic, parallelism, and correct form.

STEP 6

Write the First Draft

You might spend some class time going over the "What You Do Not Have to Do" list on page 71 and the general guidelines on page 72. Emphasize point 2 in the general guidelines.

Transforming stacks of note cards into a first draft is a daunting task that challenges even the brightest students. Some students deal with the difficulty of the task by procrastinating. Either they delay getting started or they write a little and then come to a complete halt. The suggested timetables on page 137 allow a week or more for drafting (unless students are on the four-week schedule, in which case they have four days). You can keep students on schedule by announcing a date when you will spot-check everyone's first draft. Basically, you need only make sure that each student's draft exists in its entirety. Do not stop to read first drafts carefully.

Since many good writers postpone writing their introductions and conclusions until after they have drafted the body of their paper, you might delay the text and exercises for the introduction (pages 73–76) and conclusion (pages 81–83) until after students draft the body. By this time, students have outlined the body of their papers twice and have worked extensively with their note cards, so they probably have a good idea of what they are going to say and the order in which they are going to say it.

Writing groups and peer editors are essential at the revising stage (Step 8), but you might also encourage students to share sections of their first drafts informally with partners or with their writing group. Assure students that after they complete their first draft, they will have completed their most difficult task.

Exercise 1

Analyzing an Introduction (page 74)

Answers will vary. Sample answers are given.
You may want to discuss the introduction and the students' answers with the class as a whole.

1. I. The characters; II. The characters' situations; III. The novels' symbols

2. The introduction is very good, but it might help if the writer told a little bit more about both novels. I have never heard of Herman Hesse's *Siddhartha*. What is it about? Is the boy an American Indian or from India? What does "spiritual fulfillment" mean?

Exercise 2

Writing an Introduction (page 75)

Answers will vary. A sample introduction is given:

A six-year-old girl is "walking" the letters that spell her name, and a seven-year-old boy is gluing macaroni to bright red paper to spell the word "love." These are two of the many young children who have reading problems. Parents can help their children with reading problems by using simple techniques and materials that appeal to four different senses: visual (sight), auditory (hearing), tactile (touch), and kinesthetic (motion).

Exercise 3

Drafting Your Introduction (page 76)

Introductions will vary. Students should be encouraged to exercise an evaluation of their own writing; no one should feel constrained to use the introduction chosen by the peer reviewers.

Whenever students evaluate anything, ask them to try to give reasons to support their evaluations. As the peer reviewers give feedback on the introductions they prefer, ask them to give a reason for their preference.

Exercise 4

What's Wrong with This Paragraph? (page 78)

Answers will vary. Sample answers are given.

1. It is hard to tell from this one paragraph. The paper seems to be about primates.

2. Many primates have been trained to perform as humans do.

3. Yes, but a quotation would be a good addition. The paragraph contains the writer's personal experience (inappropriate for a research paper), statistics, and examples.

4. The writer does not indicate the source of the facts and statistics. Documentation is missing from the paragraph.

Exercise 5

Writing a Paragraph (page 79)

Before students get started on this exercise, emphasize that they are not to use all of the information given. They are to write a single paragraph based on part of the notes. Require them to check their paragraphs for complete sentences and for coherence. Students' paragraphs will vary considerably, and it would be helpful to discuss them in class. You might divide students into small groups to read and comment on each other's paragraphs. A sample paragraph is given:

Quetzalcoatl, the ancient Mexican god of agriculture, science, and the arts, left his people in a way that is similar to the way King Arthur left his people. Both sailed away in a boat across a large body of water. Quetzalcoatl was exiled and left on a raft made of snakes, vowing to return some day. King Arthur, the legendary founder of Camelot, sailed away on a barge to the isle of Avalon, promising to return when Britain needed him.

Exercise 6

Writing the Body of Your Research Paper (page 80)

Answers will vary. The point of the self-evaluation questions is to reinforce the idea that the draft is not the final version. Students who procrastinate often turn in a research paper they have just drafted without allowing adequate time for revision and proofreading. You can avoid this problem by requiring that students turn in a draft (so that you can review it briefly) by a certain date, well before the final paper is due. Before students draft the body of the paper, you might briefly review the questions posed in this exercise. Assure them that there are no "correct" answers. They need not feel constrained to follow the final outline exactly (item 4) or use all of their note cards (item 5).

Exercise 7

Analyzing a Conclusion (page 82)

This conclusion has a challenging vocabulary and a sophisticated writing style. It should be accessible to most high school students. However, if you are dealing with younger students or a class with limited abilities, choose a simpler conclusion (from one of students' papers from previous years) to analyze.

Answers will vary. Sample answers are given. In class, discuss students' answers and the conclusion itself.

1. The two selections are probably Roethke's life and Roethke's work.

2. The conclusion would be better without the long Boyers quote because it is difficult to understand.

3. The writer might make the sentences a little shorter and easier to understand. Instead of a quotation by a critic, it would be good to end the paper with an appropriate quotation from a Roethke poem.

Exercise 8

Writing a Conclusion for Your Research Paper (page 83)

Ask students to add a sentence or two telling why they chose this conclusion.

Exercise 9

Using Quotations (page 85)

Answers will vary. Have the students meet in small groups to compare their answers. Assure them that there are no "right" answers to this exercise. Sample answers are given. Note that in a real paper each of the sentences would include a reference (in parentheses) to a bibliography source card number.

1. Who can ever forget King's voice proclaiming his great hope: "I have a dream that one day this nation will rise up and live out the true meaning of its creed...."

2. In Shakespeare's *Hamlet*, Polonius gives Laertes good advice: "...to thine own self be true,... Thou canst not then be false to any man."

3. "There are only two or three human stories," wrote the American novelist Willa Cather, "and they go on repeating themselves as fiercely as if they had never happened before."

Document Sources

This chapter details the MLA style of parenthetical citation, which most English teachers prefer. Although the chapter covers all of the most common kinds of sources students will use, some students may need to document a type of source not covered on pages 89–92. Try to have in class one copy of the MLA Handbook for Writers of Research Papers, *Fourth Edition (1995)*, for students to refer to. This style manual gives rules and examples for more kinds of sources than a Ph.D. thesis writer can possibly use. Even though it has an index, students are likely to need help in using the MLA Handbook *to locate information.*

Remind students that Appendix B in this text shows how to document sources using three different styles: the APA style, the MLA style for footnotes, and the MLA style for endnotes. Specify clearly which style you want students to use in their papers.

Exercise 1

What's Wrong with These Citations?
(page 92)

Go over the directions in class, emphasizing that students will not need to use all of the information given. Suggest they double-check their answers, referring to the rules for citations. You might have them discuss their answers in a small group.

1. Also, Alice and Siddhartha both went through an initiation, an increased awareness of the world. For Alice, it was when she realized that the Queen and her court were "nothing but a pack of cards" (ch. 12), not authority figures to be respected and obeyed without question. [Students may also place the citation at the end of the sentence, before the period.]

2. For Siddhartha, the initiation came when he stopped believing that the world was illusory and superficial, when he saw that "Meaning and reality were not hidden somewhere behind things, they were in them, in all of them" (Hesse 32).

Exercise 2

Be a Peer Editor (page 93)

Students' answers should *not* vary from the answers shown here:

The poetry of Theodore Roethke (1908–1963) has other literary influences. Stanley Kunitz notes "throwbacks" to nursery rhymes, folk literature, counting songs, the Bible, and Blake. "But," he adds, "the poems, original and incomparable, belong to the poet and not his sources" (Kunitz 102–103). A further influence is the poetry of both T. S. Eliot and W. B. Yeats. In Roethke's *Words for the Wind*, for instance, the poem "The Dying Man" is "in a voice almost indistinguishable from Yeats's" (Snodgrass 104–105). Some critics have attacked Roethke's imitation of Yeats, calling it a sign of weakness on Roethke's part and a lack of his own ideas and insight (Mills 30).

Roethke's poems are intensely personal. He takes the evolution of self as a theme in much of his poetry, occasionally relating it to another, or a beloved (Mills 30–31). An example of the self theme is found in the poem "Open House":

> My secrets cry aloud.
> I have no need for tongue.
> My heart keeps open house,
> My doors are widely swung.
> An epic of the eyes
> My love, with no disguise. (1–6)

Exercise 3

Writing Parenthetical Citations (page 94)

Students' answers should *not* vary. Go over the answers in class and make sure students understand which rule applies to each answer.

1. (Herzog 120)
2. ("Eskimo")
3. ("Habit")
4. (Strauss)
5. (Langley and Fox xxxi–xxxiii) or (Langley and Fox xxxi–iii)
6. (Wilson)
7. (173–181)
8. ("Elegy for Jane" 14–17)

Exercise 4

Writing Parenthetical Citations for Your Paper (page 95)

Before students start, make sure they understand exactly what they are being asked to do. They will need to replace the place-holding references to their bibliography source cards with the appropriate citation as per the style rules given in this chapter. As preparation for this task, you might go over several examples in class.

Exercise 5

What's Wrong with Each of the Following Works Cited Entries? (page 97)

Students' answers should *not* vary.

1. Williams, Trevor. The History of Invention. New York: Facts on File, 1987.
2. DuPree, David. "Top Crop of Free Agents Ripe for Picking." USA Today. 9 July 1996: 3C.
3. Conaway, James. The Smithsonian: 150 Years of Adventure, Discovery, and Wonder. New York: Knopf, 1995.
4. McGinn, Daniel. "I Spy a '98 Corvette." Newsweek. 15 July 1996: 40–41.
5. Kramer, Jack. The World Wildlife Fund Book of Orchids. New York: Abbeville Press, 1989.
6. Futsher, Vicki. E-Mail to the author. 14 Dec. 1999.

Exercise 6

Writing Your Works Cited List (page 98)

Ask students to review the model Works Cited list on pages 96–97 before they begin this exercise and refer to this model and the rules on pages 87–92 as they prepare their own Works Cited list. Partners can double-check alphabetization and style. It would be helpful to have in the classroom one or more copies of the *MLA Handbook* for students to consult if they need further help.

Before students begin this chapter, make sure they understand the difference between revising and proofreading. Revising (Step 8) involves making changes in the paper's content and organization in order to improve the first draft. Proofreading (Step 9) involves identifying and correcting errors in spelling, capitalization, punctuation, grammar, usage, and documentation.

Most teachers will agree that revising is the most frequently neglected stage of student writing. For a typical writing assignment (not the research paper), many students turn in a first draft they have written late the night before and never glanced at again. Since it is virtually impossible for any writer to focus on everything at the same time, this chapter breaks the revising task into five separate readings: (1) meeting teacher requirements, (2) unity, (3) coherence, (4) sentences, and (5) word choice. Assure students that if they approach revising in this methodical way, focusing on one aspect at a time, you can guarantee that they will improve their first drafts immeasurably.

Peer editing and writing groups play a crucial role in the revising process, but you might hold off having students read and comment on each other's drafts until each writer completes his or her own revisions. Ask peer editors to follow the same approach: focusing separately on unity, coherence, sentences, and word choice.

Practice in combining sentences (see page 108) has proved an effective way to improve student writing. If you have time, give students additional instruction and practice in sentence combining.

Exercise 1

What's Wrong with This Paragraph? (page 102)

Students will benefit from doing the exercise individually and then meeting with small groups to compare and discuss their revisions. Students' answers will vary somewhat. A sample answer has the following changes:

1. Cross out: "(about 20 poisonous snakes out of the 120 species)"

2. Begin a new paragraph with the words: "In many localities, especially in India, …"

3. Cross out: "More than 20,000 deaths in India each year are attributed to the bite of poisonous snakes."

4. Cross out: "In Europe, white storks are also considered good luck, and people build platforms on their roofs so storks will build their nests there (Columbia 2628)."

5. Cross out: " 'Of course,' Hegner reports, 'accidents *do* happen, and some people who step carelessly are bitten and die.' " [Students may make a case for keeping this sentence.]

6. Cross out: "My cousin Jerrod stepped on a black snake once, but nothing happened to him."

Exercise 2

Revising for Unity (page 104)

After students have revised their drafts for unity, have them exchange papers with a partner. Each partner should read the draft, focusing only on unity. Caution peer editors to restrict their comments and responses to unity.

Exercise 3

Revising for Coherence (page 106)

This is a challenging exercise that you might do with the class as a whole, stopping to discuss suggested changes. Note that the paragraph is about the cause of dreams, so sentence 1 has been omitted in the revision. At the end of the paragraph, short, choppy sentences have been combined. Transitional words and phrases (in italics) have been added. Students' answers will vary. A sample revision is given:

No one knows for sure what causes dreams, but scientists have different theories. Some psychologists think that dreams are a window into the subconscious, an important sign of inner thoughts and buried feelings (4). Sigmund Freud, *for example*, believed that dreams represent wish-fulfillments. Others insist that dreams are a forgetting process, a way to get rid of unwanted or annoying emotions. Scientists Francis Crick and Graeme Mitchison, *for instance*, believe that dreams are an "unlearning process by which the brain rids itself of unwanted impulses and associations" (5). They believe that complex networks of cells in the cerebral cortex form faulty connections that give rise to fantasies, obsessions, and hallucinations when people are awake. When people sleep, *however*, the cortex is cut off from its normal input and output, and the lower brain sends random impulses, which cause dreams (6).

Exercise 4

Revising for Coherence (page 106)

Remind students that their goal is to make their ideas easier to understand. Besides inserting transitional words and phrases, students should consider adding definitions, explaining terms, and substituting easier words for more difficult ones. Suggest that they hold off exchanging papers with partners until they've completed Exercise 5.

Exercise 5

Revising Sentences (page 108)

Students' answers will vary considerably. A sample revision is given below. Comparing revisions in small groups will help students see that there are many possible ways to revise a weak paragraph. Students may become aware of options that they never even considered while revising the paragraph.

One of the great contributors to psychology was the American psychologist B. F. Skinner, who lived from 1904 to 1990. Skinner, a behavioral psychologist, believed that psychologists should study human behavior instead of focusing on concepts that can not be observed. He believed that behavior can be shaped or learned with positive reinforcement, such as praise and rewards. According to Skinner, behavior can also be shaped with negative reinforcement, such as punishment and yelling.

Exercise 6

Revising Everything There Is to Revise (page 110)

Again, students' answers will vary. A sample answer is given below. If students have discussed Exercise 5 revisions in small groups, you might want to discuss this exercise with the class as a whole. One way to do this would be to go over the paragraph sentence by sentence and ask for several volunteers to tell how they revised each sentence. You might note with students that this revision uses present tense verbs to describe the action in the novel. This convention, used in writing about literature, is called the "literary present."

Mark Twain's A Connecticut Yankee in King Arthur's Court is about Hank Morgan, a foreman in an arms factory in 19th-century Hartford, Connecticut. During a fight, a man named Hercules hits Morgan with a crowbar, and Morgan wakes to find himself in sixth-century England during the time of

King Arthur. When Morgan sets out to bring 19th-century civilization to King Arthur's court, he comes into conflict with an old man named Merlin, who is court magician to Arthur. Morgan also comes into conflict with the ignorance and superstition of the ordinary people. On its surface, A Connecticut Yankee in King Arthur's Court appears to be a light, humorous adventure story, but it is much more than that. In this novel Twain parodies medieval English chivalry and romance. The novel also attacks social unfairness, political injustice, human ignorance and superstition.

Exercise 7

Revising Sentences in Your Draft
(page 111)

This is the third go-round on revising their drafts; students have already revised for unity (Exercise 2) and coherence (Exercise 4). Hold off peer editing (exchanging papers with partners) until after they complete the fourth go-round on diction, or word choice (Exercise 9). By that time, their drafts should show many revisions. Remind students that this is almost the last step before writing the final version of their papers.

Exercise 8

Focusing on Word Choice (page 111)

Answers will vary. A sample answer is given. Before students focus on word choice in their own papers (Exercise 9), it would be helpful to discuss this exercise with the class as a whole. You might use an overhead projector to show this sample answer, or ask for volunteers to read their revisions. Assure students that there is no single "right" way to revise a paragraph; many different revisions are possible.

Imagine that you have handed over your money to Mr. Sam, an accountant with an excellent reputation. Mr. Sam claims he will invest your money so that when you retire, you will have a pension for your old age. However, you learn one day that Mr. Sam has been using your pension money for his own purposes. He has been paying his bills, buying electronic equipment, and making loans to his friends; but he assures you that he will repay your money with interest when you need it. Would you be comfortable giving your money to Mr. Sam? If you have a job, Uncle Sam is doing all of these things with your money. Social Security funds are being used to pay government bills, to build weapons, and to make loans to foreign countries. To understand the uproar regarding the Social Security Trust Fund and its future, it is necessary to know the background of this crucial and controversial issue.

Exercise 9

Revising for Word Choice (page 112)

Remind students that word choice creates the tone of writing and that they are to create a formal tone. Using precise words for general ones not only helps communicate an idea clearly, but also tends to eliminate wordiness. It is time—at last—to have students exchange their marked-up drafts with partners for feedback. If the drafts are illegible and students have used a computer, ask them to make their corrections and print a fresh copy of the revised draft.

STEP 9
Proofread

This chapter breaks proofreading into several separate readings: spelling, capitalization, punctuation, grammar and usage, and documentation. This methodical approach to proofreading not only makes students more aware of the kinds of errors they should be looking for but also increases the number of errors students identify and correct. Remind students that a research paper should have a formal tone and be written according to the conventions of standard English. In this connection, stress that contractions are not suitable to such papers. If you have not already done so, assemble a small reference library containing several college dictionaries and copies of a good grammar, usage, and mechanics handbook. Encourage students to use these reference books whenever they think something "looks funny."

If you plan to teach language mini-lessons throughout the school year, here are the "writer's grammar" topics to emphasize:

- complete sentences, fragments, run-on sentences
- subject-verb agreement
- irregular verb forms
- irregular comparisons
- clear pronoun reference

Provide students with practice exercises and worksheets for every mini-lesson.

Exercise 1

Proofreading for Spelling Errors
(page 116)

Students' answers should *not* vary. The following corrections should be made:

In Paragraph 1
    Sentence 1: shown, connection

    Sentence 2: movement, occur

    Sentence 3: there, breathing

    Sentence 4: anywhere, ninety, occurs

In Paragraph 2
    Sentence 1: patients

    Sentence 2: Researchers, patients, movements

    Sentence 3: extremely, irritable, received

    Sentence 4: nights, allowed

    Sentence 5: normally

    Sentence 6: previous

Exercise 2

Checking the Spelling in Your Final Draft
(page 117)

If there is time, students might exchange papers with partners to double-check their spelling. Students should still be working on their first draft as they do this exercise. In Step 10, they are reminded to proofread their final drafts before turning them in.

Exercise 3

Creating a Personal Proofreading Log
(page 117)

Students' proofreading logs may be kept in a separate part of their notebook, a folder, or a little notebook. Urge them to keep their logs up-to-date and to review them before they begin the final draft. Besides having students record each word's correct spelling and their misspelling, you might also ask students to record *why* they misspelled the word. Thinking about why they made the mistake will locate the "trouble spot" and help them avoid repeating the same mistake.

Exercise 4

Proofreading a Paragraph (page 118)

Students' answers should *not* vary. You might go over this exercise in class. The following corrections should be made:

Sentence 1: Piece, American, Richard Wilbur

Sentence 2: In, guardians, of art, (1.3).

Sentence 3: hovering, valuable, museum, pieces

Sentence 4: Wilbur, (1.3), piece, art, its

Sentence 5: though, suspicious, French

Sentence 6: do not (not *don't*), whether, piece

Sentence 7: art, carefully

Sentence 8: There, attitude

Sentence 9: museum's, hallways

Exercise 5

Proofreading Your Final Draft for Punctuation (page 119)

Students may have some questions about matters of punctuation not covered in the chapter. Answer their questions directly or, if they are capable of finding the answers themselves, refer them to a handbook of grammar and usage.

Exercise 6

What Is Wrong with These Sentences? (page 120)

Answers may vary somewhat. Sample answers are given. Point out that in an actual paper, there would be parenthetical citations for quoted material.

1. Henry David Thoreau, one of America's leading philosophers, was a friend of Ralph Waldo Emerson, the essayist and poet.

2. In 1845 Thoreau built a small wooden cabin on the shore of Walden Pond, where he lived for almost two years.

3. Of course, one of the reasons he went to Walden Pond was to experience its incredible beauty. He describes this beauty in Walden, his book based on the very detailed journal he kept while he lived in the cabin.

4. Thoreau had deeper motives than merely appreciation of nature's beauty. He believed, as Emerson did, that nature reflects the inner self and teaches us much about life.

5. In Walden Thoreau tells of meeting a poor woodcutter, who had very few material things but possessed a love of nature and was honest, simple, and content.

6. The essayist E. B. White called Walden "the only book I own." White said that he kept Thoreau's book handy "for relief" during times of despair.

7. In the conclusion to Walden, Thoreau wrote, "If a man does not keep pace with his companions, perhaps it is because he hears a different drummer. Let him step to the music which he hears, however measured or far away."

8. Thoreau also wrote these words: "If one advances confidently in the direction of his dreams, and endeavors to live the life which he has imagined, he will meet with a success unexpected in common hours."

9. In his essay "Civil Disobedience," published in 1849, Thoreau explains why he refused to pay the Massachusetts poll tax.

10. Both Mahatma Gandhi, leader of India's struggle for independence from Britain, and Dr. Martin Luther King, Jr., American civil rights leader, were inspired by Thoreau's essay.

Exercise 7

Proofreading Your Final Draft (page 122)

If students have done Exercises 2 (spelling) and 5 (punctuation), they need only focus on grammar and usage for this exercise.

Exercise 8

Proofreading—One Last Look (page 123)

Assure students that "neatness counts." Make clear in advance how many corrections you consider acceptable in their final papers.

STEP 10

Prepare the Final Manuscript

This chapter contains no exercises because students have had all the instruction and practice they need to produce their final drafts. It's a good idea to go over the paper's form in class and answer any questions that students may have. You might assign students to read the student model paper on pages 126–136 as homework and then spend some time the next day talking about the student model and going over the annotations.